MADRE

Jessica Chapnik Kahn

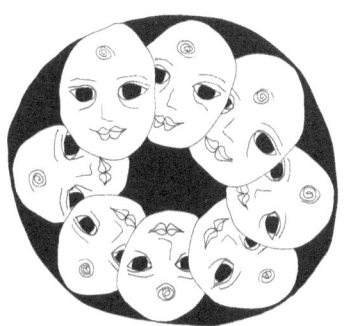

For my mother,
Elisa Chapnik,
and my father,
Leonardo Chapnik.
It is an honour to be your daughter.
Thank you. For everything.

For my son
Lev Vishnu Kahn.
You are my poem.
Thank you for making me yours.
I love you.

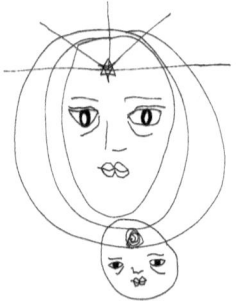

First published 2019 by Mother Courage
This edition published 2023 by The Forces Four Us

Poems and illustrations
© Jessica Chapnik Kahn 2019

Published by The Forces Four Us
www.theforcesfourus.com

TABLE OF CONTENTS

xi	Foreword
1	First Music
2	The Altar of Love
3	The Loneliness Is Deep
4	Morning is the Most Compassionate Time
5	Kol D'Mama
6	Divine Light
7	Mother, You Are the First Guru
8	I Have Completely Disappeared
9	Sometimes Your Eyes Look Black
11	Weary Eden
12	Sacred Text
13	Woman Forgotten
14	At the Breast (Part 1)
15	At the Breast (Part 2)
16	The Little Train from My Childhood
17	Shabbat
18	Let Eden Be
19	Fox at Heart
21	I Am the Fruit
22	Sleeping Mother
23	Wish I Was You
24	Leaves, You Look Like My Baby

25	First Language
26	When This Breast Dries Up
27	I Become a Virgin
28	Waves
29	We Are a Meditation
31	I Am a Forest
32	The Least Lonely Feeling
33	Mother in Your Heart
34	Be Tender with This Mystery
35	Just Like You
36	The Holy Spirit Is a Broken Woman
37	God Chooses the Lonely
39	I Heard Him in the Garden
40	Holy Fire Feels Like Hell
41	My Volcano Is Lit
42	Milk
43	You Are God's Anatomy
44	The Thing That Cuts Me the Most
45	Lovingly, the Garden Ends
46	No Matter Where He Goes
49	Every Win Is for You
50	Teach Me the Secret of Your Fire
51	This Is Radiance
52	Touching Is Everything
54	We Are Still
57	Mother, Father, Why Do You Cry?

58	Come to Mother
59	You Were Not Born Naked
60	Love Quashes the Flesh
62	You Remind Me of a Folk Song
63	Make Me a Dove
65	When the Future Comes
66	This is How Seeds Grow
67	My Dreams Are All Dead
68	The Language of the Holy Spirit
69	Impossible Teacher
70	Return to Love
71	You Know Me from the Inside
72	Weakened in All My Strengths
74	Growing in the Night
75	A Burning Bush
76	The Breast Possesses Me
77	Shard in Your Hand
78	One Beautiful Moment
79	Waterlily Garden
80	From the Light of My Heart
82	My Womb Is Egypt
83	This Is Called Desire
84	To Be Born You Have to Trudge Through Filth
85	I Love Him in a Garden
86	The Feeling of His Shining
87	Paradise Is at the Feet of Mother

89	It's Right to Be Alone
90	Little Bird
91	Higher Mother
92	Failure, You Make Me Proud
93	The Snake Made Us Eat
94	You've Made Me Forget My Own Beauty
95	You Are Still Fragrant
96	If You Hear a Bird
98	Many Things Must Die
99	You Have Many Secret Names
100	Imprint of You
101	All My Wrong Becomes a Flower
102	Milk Is More Real Than Rain
104	In the World Yet to Come
106	The Lord Always Hears a Cry in the Night
107	I Feel Her Magnet
108	You Must Not Know Yourself
109	Lionheart
110	I Wish You Thought I Was Beautiful
112	This Is Where We Meet
114	His River Is Not Filled with Water
115	I Am a Vine
116	I Found Him in a Basket
117	A Mystery I Can't Remember Now
118	I Will Never Pray With My Eyes Closed Again
119	You Belong to the Feminine

ILLUSTRATIONS

i	*Mother Lakshmi*
iii	*Tikkun Olam*
iv	*Remembering Our Dreams*
xiii	*Harini*
10	*Baby on the Breast*
14	*The Flowers He Picks for Me at the End of the Day*
20	*Our Lady of the Sacred Lev*
23	*Seashell*
30	*Lakshmi Baby*
36	*Holy Feet*
38	*A Baby, a Cobra*
42	*Lakshmi Breasts*
48	*All the Parts of His Soul*
51	*He Drinks All of My Nature*
56	*Belly in a Belly in the Belly of the Whale*
59	*Mother's Milk, Mother's Tears*
64	*Study of His Face*
73	*The Feeling of His Shining*
79	*My View*
81	*Baby Vishnu*
85	*His Nature*
88	*His Cry*
97	*Vishnu's Navel*
100	*Milk Moon*
103	*Sustaining the Sustainer*
111	*I Dreamed That He Fit in the Palm of My Hand*
118	*Baby Buddha*

FOREWORD

I began writing this book with my son at my breast, in the first few days of his life. I did not intend on writing a book. There was no further thought from my mind. I simply began to understand his face by drawing him. I began to understand my experience of him by writing. We were being born at exactly the same time. It was an exquisite, difficult bliss.

There were many visits in those months from the people I love. But when the house became silent, when it was just my son and I, undistracted at the breast, the words and pictures would come. They came so softly and quietly. They made me feel so human.

In India, quite a few years ago now, I spoke to a wise, learned man considered by many to be a saint. We spoke about children and about my fears around ever becoming a mother. He said to me, 'All of creation is a mother. The ants are mothers. Even men are mothers. You yourself are already a mother, you always have been. What are you afraid of?'

I am thankful for these poems. Writing them has helped me realise the mother within me. I hope that in reading them, they have their own unique way with you. We all came from a womb. We all return to it. Mother is within us all. This is my love song.

FIRST MUSIC

The first music I ever heard
Was your breathing
Tender against my naked breast.

The first thing that ever pierced me
Were your black, bewildered eyes
Tugging at my narrow, newborn heart.

THE ALTAR OF LOVE

Everyday
I arrive
At the altar of love
With my eternity
Maternity
Ragged and asleep
Take me as I am
Help me in my devotion

THE LONELINESS IS DEEP

The loneliness is deep
Even in my happiest moments with you

The days are short
But the night hours burn
Like prickly flames that have no warmth
Or kindness

I want to be held
But now my arms are for holding
I want to ask
But now my voice is for answering

I bury my face
In your neck
In your clothes
In your hair
Loneliness never smelt so sweet

MORNING IS THE MOST COMPASSIONATE TIME

Morning is the most compassionate time
when I am a gentle doe. I give him rain.
I give him light. And when darkness comes,
my life takes flight. I become a man
empowered by the night.

KOL D'MAMA

It's not in the mountain
Where sages retire

Not in the quake
That purges the liar

Not in the wind
Where spirits conspire

Not in the lover
Who inflamed my desire

Not in the lightning
That aches to be fire

Not in the flame
The great purifier

It's in his still small voice
Rising out of the mire

That is the breath
That takes the mother higher

DIVINE LIGHT

Why is your divine light
Not enough
To extinguish
My deepest dark?

MOTHER, YOU ARE THE FIRST GURU

Mother, you are the first guru
From an ocean of milk
You extend
Pretend
You have no idea
(Yet)
What it means to be
Everything

I HAVE COMPLETELY DISAPPEARED

In some mysterious way
I have completely disappeared.
What makes me despair
Is that I like it.

SOMETIMES YOUR EYES LOOK BLACK

Sometimes your eyes look black to me
Like your oceans turned to nighttime

I tell everyone you understand everything
But when we fight in front of you
It's easy to pretend you understand nothing

This is how we adults are, baby
Confused by the way things are
Drinking wine to keep us sober
Wanting, wanting no one thing

My heart is like the last light of dusk
It fights to stay
Or is it free
To fade away?

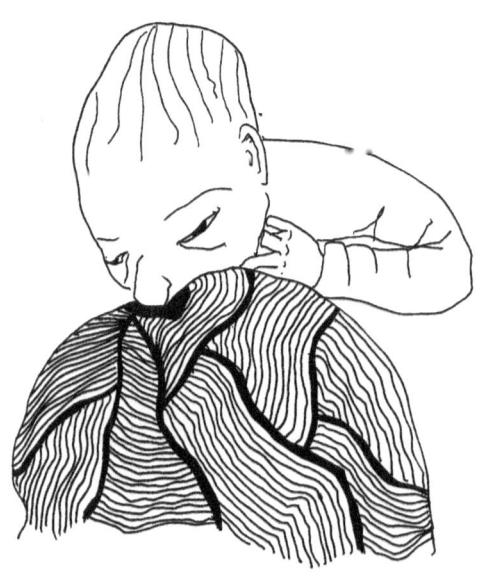

WEARY EDEN

I am two shrivelled fruits
With many branches
He hangs off me
Sucking, laughing, crying
Milk dripping like tears
He becomes everything he needs to be
In my weary Eden

SACRED TEXT

I've faded
Washed myself out
In the rain
Like a god
Like a plant
My roots are a sacred text
I am a leaf, longing

WOMAN FORGOTTEN

I sweep through the house
Like a hurricane
Eyes like a dim night light
Hair like live wires
Heart heavy full
Melted metal

He calls out to me
To who I am
Who I was
Woman forgotten
Woman irrelevant
Discarded, unknown

I lift his perfection
Into my arms
Corrupt and clumsy
I strive to give him light

AT THE BREAST
(Part 1)

He forgets who he is
At the breast
Hands thumping my chest
His eyes an eclipse
Oblivion

AT THE BREAST
(Part 2)

He remembers who he is
At the breast
Mind at rest
Our heartbeat, found
Eternity

THE LITTLE TRAIN FROM MY CHILDHOOD

Sitting alone on the grass
By the beach
With the little train from my childhood
I had to
Run away from you
Because for the first time
I felt you'd do better without me
Because for the first time
I felt I'd do better without you
My bones hurt from your dependence
My skin aches from where your mouth pressed

SHABBAT

In the name
Of the extinguished flame
That is
Complete service
I pray:
Fire.
Work.

LET EDEN BE

Please don't tell him
That apple is apple
And fall is fall
Let him be one
With all things
For a moment longer
Resist your temptation
To teach him
Distance
I beg of you
Trust his emptiness
Let Eden be

FOX AT HEART

Like a star
I sleep and shine
Return the apple
In my eye
Just a moment of disbelief
Where I drank
And sank in grief
Everything I thought was true
Is just a tiny flame to you
Baby I'm a fox at heart
I feed you milk
While I tear things apart

I AM THE FRUIT

I am the fruit
That is the world
Eaten and bitten
By his needy mouth
Bruised and crushed
By his animal fingers
That fumble and burrow
In the deep of the night

I am the apple
That laughs at the tree
Kissing the ground
On which I lie
Happy to be
Everything he needs
Defeated at being
Someone's everything

SLEEPING MOTHER

Sleeping mother
That never sleeps
Dreamless
You look to the sea to arouse you
But only find
Seashells

WISH I WAS YOU

Here I am, baby
To touch you
Quench you
Reach you
Just for one moment;
I wish I was you.

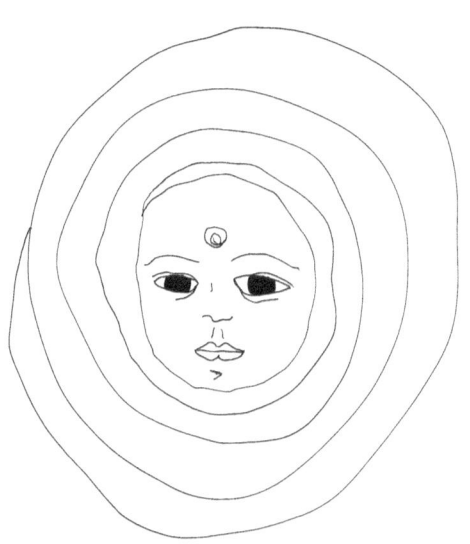

LEAVES, YOU LOOK LIKE MY BABY

Leaves,
You look
Just like
My baby
Same almond eyes
Half playful,
Half sorry,
For this fallen universe

FIRST LANGUAGE

I sing you the ocean
She calls you deep
It's our first language
It's where we meet

WHEN THIS BREAST DRIES UP

When this breast dries up
Will there always be
Invisible threads
Of primordial milk
That we once shared?

I BECOME A VIRGIN

Now and then
I become
A virgin
Closed
Bearing
And full of strange folds
In bloom
Eventually
Not quite yet
Coming

WAVES

Waves
You make me
A crumpled human
Beaten and broken
Into the sand
Like pieces of shell
That you gather
Into your arms
Like only a mother can
I trust you, I have to

WE ARE A MEDITATION

We are a meditation
You and me
Nowhere to go
Nowhere to be
Our thoughts so silent
While you laugh at the leaves
Is this what it's like
To be perfectly free?
I am a humble branch
Dying, in your garden of trees

I AM A FOREST

I am a forest of twigs
Trapped in your hair
The roots of a tree
Adorning your chest
Let me quench you
With rain, with weeping
Gods live in these leaves
Tamed, feasting

THE LEAST LONELY FEELING

All alone
With you
Is the least lonely feeling
With others
I am a blade of grass
Listening until my mouth is dry
Talking until I strain my ears
Stumbling to the door
For goodbyes, embraces
Limp from the bitter solitude

MOTHER IN YOUR HEART

Darkness
Is a higher light
A delicate beckoning
A bitter closeness
That conceals your face
And sets you apart
It should happen to you
It is not wrong
Look!
It is Mother in your heart

BE TENDER WITH THIS MYSTERY

Be tender with this mystery
Ascend unknowingly

We live among shards of glass
To stay alive inside obscurity

JUST LIKE YOU

I used to know my life
But I too have been moved
From water to air
In one sudden exile
Just like you

THE HOLY SPIRIT IS A BROKEN WOMAN

The holy spirit is a broken woman
Who makes our bodies wise
She rests so quietly on our flesh
And speaks through the soft of our thighs

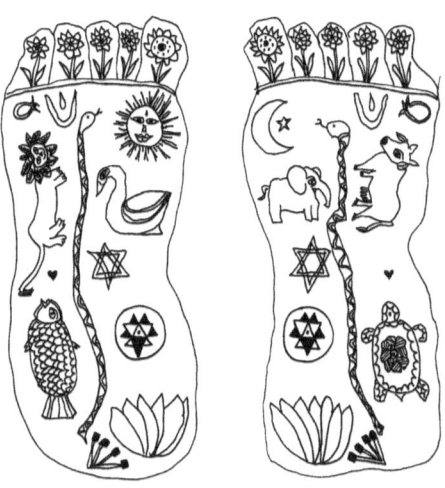

GOD CHOOSES THE LONELY

God chooses the lonely
To show her fire
A flame that devours
Your every desire

She consumes your grief
Blackens your wrong
Attends to your fever
With a mother's song

Come! Lie in her logs
Eat of her ashes
Sleep in her bosom
While your sweet baby dances

I HEARD HIM IN THE GARDEN

I heard him in the garden
While I was deep in sleep
He put his hand right through me
And pulled out a shining rib
He closed my flesh with needles
He left the wound so fresh
And when I woke
He was in my arms
A vital, tangled mess
Bone of my bones
Flesh of my flesh
Man was taken out of woman
And I saw that I was naked
And I felt no need for shame

HOLY FIRE FEELS LIKE HELL

Holy fire
Feels like hell
But damn it licks you
Likes you
When it burns
Like a friend
Who gives you strength
To carry on

MY VOLCANO IS LIT

My volcano is lit. The cries of my boy fill me with tears that don't run down my cheeks. His father tries and tries. But I am the only one and my nerves are broken. Did my mother feel these feelings? Did she feel the tension between running and loving? Did I lie in a cot while they fought and fought, wounded and fatigued by their grown-up failure?

MILK

I worry that the milk I feed you
Carries my venom, my panic
My doubt
Can your purity purify
Contaminated breasts?

YOU ARE GOD'S ANATOMY

I dig my hands into your wounds
I crumble into my foolishness
You are God's flawless anatomy
God help my unbelief

THE THING THAT CUTS ME THE MOST

The thing that cuts me the most
Is his hunger
Those seconds before the breast
Where he becomes a desperate animal
Trembling, in my newborn hands
Without me, he is nothing
A mirror of my own wretchedness
All this, an instant before
Everything wonderful comes

LOVINGLY, THE GARDEN ENDS

I try to let him have his bliss
But time moves on
The orgasm, the womb, the breast
We can never exist there for long
God throws us out suddenly
Lovingly, the garden ends
We are born with that death within us
To find ourselves again

NO MATTER WHERE HE GOES

No matter where he goes,
His world always returns to me
He is the branch of a tree
Growing from my tender hip

*

Here I am, bound to him with glorious love
Longing for everything out there
Oh to be important again

*

I can no longer remember any part of my life
All my memories are gone
Maybe this is happiness, but it's hard to know

*

Death is a dream we don't understand
God is as mysterious as the breast
In sustaining him, he sustains us

*

In my dream, my father said:
'Can you believe what God has done to me?'
When I looked at him, it was my son's face

*

There is such sorrow in letting go
Of the mother I want to be
To become the mother I have to be

*

I feel his small bones bend under my rough fingers
My hands are clumsy
Every single day I hurt for him

*

To feel I have failed him is a new form of unbearable
I close my eyes to stop the feeling
But the thoughts live in the dark of my eyelids

*

I learn something new every day
When I cannot go on
There is so much more strength

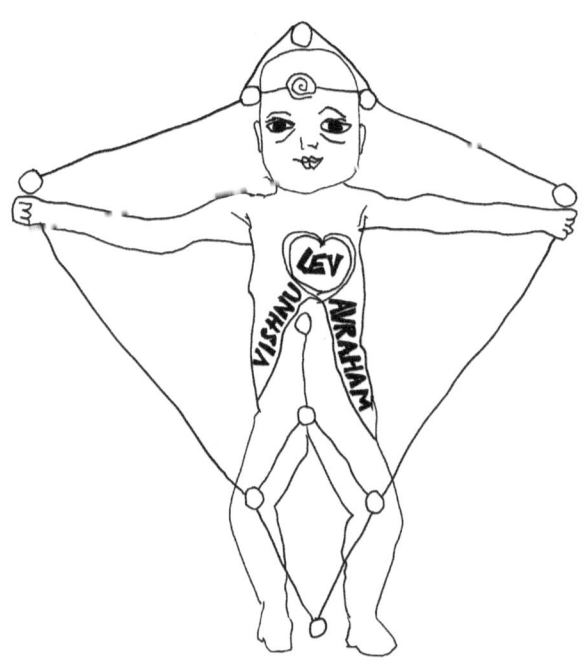

EVERY WIN IS FOR YOU

This love burns
Every day I swallow its embers
Fire tastes like water but with a razor's edge

*

When you cry, I hold onto my bones
You reach my ancient places
Before the before where I used to be dissolved

*

Milk is a way to disappear into your eyes
Fold you up
Put you back in the womb again
Make us one again

*

In foetal position, we all become babies
Naked and sown at the seams
Born with our death within us

*

I win sometimes
Now every win is for you

TEACH ME THE SECRET OF YOUR FIRE

With each divine utterance
From his mouth
My soul flies away

This temple has an eternal flame
But O to keep it ablaze
How do I hold down this holiness?
Teach me the secret of your fire

THIS IS RADIANCE

You've raised my soul
Above my body
I am upside down
My roots are in heaven
This is radiance

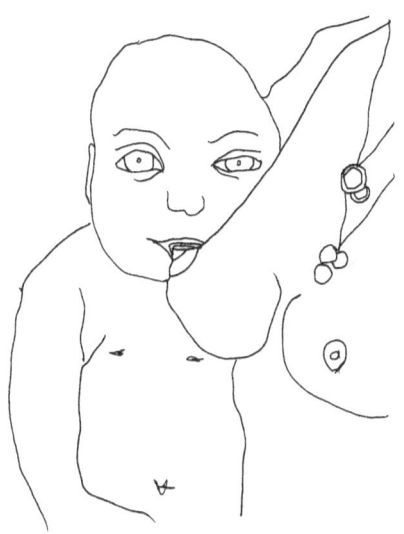

TOUCHING IS EVERYTHING

We lie ourselves down on forgiving sheets
They cry for us to be naked

*

I ask him: Can you help me find my soul?
But there is a hollowness to his best efforts

*

Sometimes lovers have the same wounds
Sometimes they take turns dying

*

I need him so much that I push him away
It hurts to depend on him
The most exhausting thing of all
Is our lack of kindness

*

It was nice for a moment to have that fire
Why do we resist the things we want?
Why do we look so beautiful when we are wrong?

*

Look how much trust you have
When you let yourself sleep
Did you know that trust was in there?

*

Certain memories make me sick
Inside all of them there is only one answer:
There is no one to blame
Save yourself

*

I thought we weren't like that
But we are like that, aren't we my love?

*

Every day, we lie to ourselves
But is it really lying
When we never knew the truth in the first place?

*

You are the great longing
I am the great aloneness
Touching is everything

WE ARE STILL

We are still
in the tower
scattered and confused

We are still
in Egypt
enslaved and abused

We are still
in the desert
aching for her kiss

We are still
in the garden
blind to our bliss

We are still
in the dark
in the womb of the whale

She delivers
us whole
for her love to take sail

We are still
in the flood
washed by her strife

O destruction
for mother
is the water of life

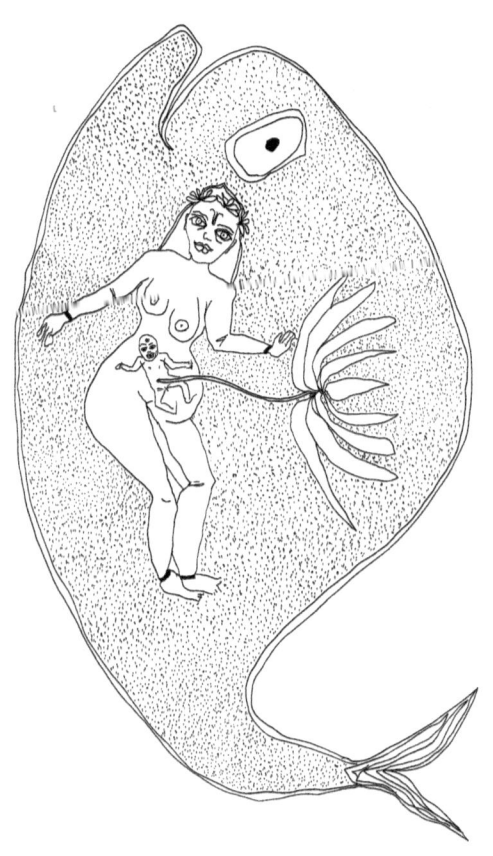

MOTHER, FATHER, WHY DO YOU CRY?

Mother, Father
Why do you cry?
Do not be confused by the bitter eye
This is his name not his name
This is his body not his body
This is your son not your son
This is just a dream of longing

COME TO MOTHER

If you want to know God
Come to mother

Let her speak
Out of your throat

You have no choice
You are the one

YOU WERE NOT BORN NAKED

You were not born naked
You were clothed in clouds of glory
When my eyes saw your light
I regained my perfect mind

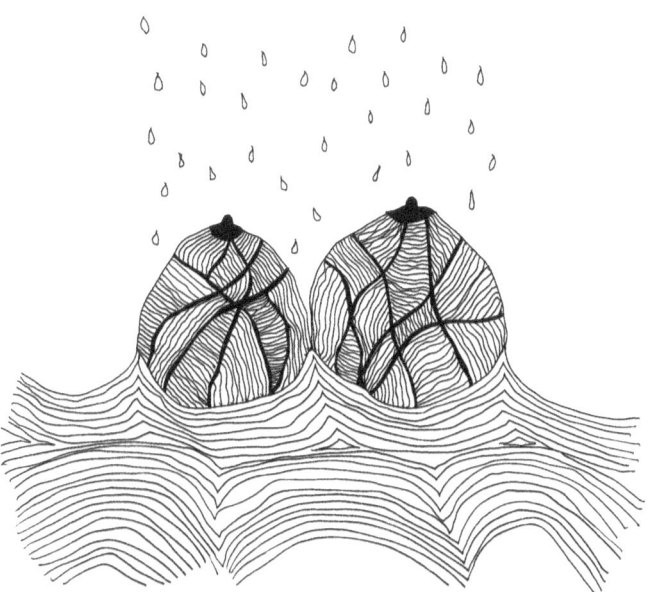

LOVE QUASHES THE FLESH

Love quashes the flesh
Throws out your nature
Digs out your death
To reveal your infinity

*

When God created you
It was with breath
With numbers, with letters

*

When I hold you
Prayers rise in me
You are saving my life
You are a city of complete

*

In my mother heart
Weeping lives on the left
And joy is lodged in the other
Even so, I am undivided

*

You are not growing
From the ground up
You are cascading slowly
From the hilltops of heaven

*

My body is a palace
I never imagined that I could be
God's dwelling place

*

One day, we will no longer run
We will sit and behold
There will be nothing left to do

*

There is a beautiful relief
At the very top of our prayers
Because there, there is nothing

*

The body isn't always
Filled with spirit
Deliver us from the deep

*

Because you are everything
I can serve you with
My anything, my everything

*

Finally
I heard your still, small voice
It was a birdsong
It was the sound of sages

YOU REMIND ME OF A FOLK SONG

You have brought me back together
My divisions were meant to be
I hear the anthems of all my lands
In your sweet, humble chorus

Baby, you are a poet
You have opened my ears
To the joy of my sadness

You remind me of a folk song

MAKE ME A DOVE

He is always here
Always coming
Waking us up
Taking us back
To the beginning
Where we were
Never masters
Only servants
For love
O make me a dove
That soars in your mind
Make me gentle
So God can guide

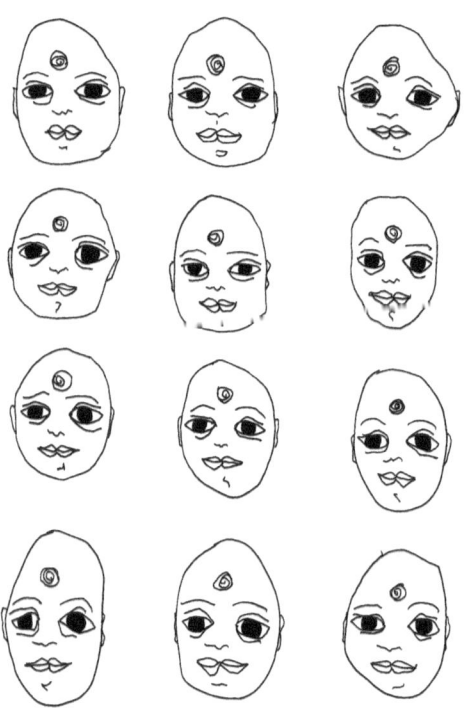

WHEN THE FUTURE COMES

When the future comes
in the middle of the night
and caresses me with invisible hands
I feel afraid

Forgive me baby
I do it to myself

Silently, I pray
in my wooden, secret heart

What kind of miracle is this
that even when I break
I survive?

THIS IS HOW SEEDS GROW

God wears darkness
Like a cloak
To hide her blinding light
This is how seeds grow
In the folds of her robes
In the womb
Of an unlit night

MY DREAMS ARE ALL DEAD

I dreamed he was rust
I dreamed he was sand
I dreamed that he fit
in the palm of my hand
I dreamed I was stone
encrusted in his chest
I dreamed that his soul
was the worms in my breast
I dreamed he was drowning
in the bottom of the ocean
I could not recover him
with my love, my devotion
I dreamed that I sewed him
with needle and thread
My visions live on
but my dreams are all dead

THE LANGUAGE OF THE HOLY SPIRIT

He speaks to us
in tongues

The language
of needing everything
and asking for nothing

The language of
trusting us
for no reason

The language of
the Holy Spirit

That drags us
by the hair
to the ground

Where on our knees
we wash his feet
with our tears
of surrender

IMPOSSIBLE TEACHER

When he sleeps, his face looks like the flowers he
picks for me at the end of the day.

I want to teach him everything I will never know.
I am his impossible teacher.

I don't want to forget what this oneness
feels like. One day, I'll need that memory.

Son is a foreign, beautiful word. Son, delight in us.

RETURN TO LOVE

Night time is the hardest when my thoughts
fall on me like buildings. I go for a walk in
the dark and let myself be afraid. My new
body makes a thud on the pavement. It wants
attention that I cannot give. Tonight, inside
my thin sleep, I will dream about dying.
But when that first light comes through my
window, when I hold your body in my hands,
all this will dissolve, and I will return to love.
I will be held and fed by heaven and all will
be all right.

YOU KNOW ME FROM THE INSIDE

No one
except God
knows me
like you do
You've seen
every organ
of my body
with your
untamed eyes
You know me
from the inside

WEAKENED IN ALL MY STRENGTHS

Weakened in all my strengths
I feel a sadness in all your victories
You learn to walk away
And begin to stare at my breast
With no hunger
Only words
My arms reach out more
Grow more
Try
But you are a mighty force of only forward
And I must meet you there
Rejoicing, rejoicing with every ache

GROWING IN THE NIGHT

I can hear him
Triumphant
Growing in the night
It is the peeling back
Of the petals of a flower
That with each painful bloom
Cry out

A BURNING BUSH

A flickering flame
In the heart of a womb
That burns and burns
But is not consumed

A baby grows
In Sinai
The holy ground
On which I lie

I am scattered on streets
I am blood on your door
God chose the grief
Of a desert floor

There is no escape
From your merciful push
Thrust me toward
A burning bush

THE BREAST POSSESSES ME

The breast possesses me
Consumes me
With eternal moments
Of perfect rapture
Absolute pain
I must have wanted to give myself away
I must have wanted it
I just didn't know it

SHARD IN YOUR HAND

Press me, mash me
Pound out my greed
Until the stone of me
Turns to clay
I am a vase
A shard in your hand
A shell made of glass
Shattering

ONE BEAUTIFUL MOMENT

People say I'm small
but I bore you
pulled you out
with my bare animal hands

*

Night and day
I wonder if I'm ruining you
but am relieved when I see the light
coming out from under your fingertips

*

When the ocean breaks on me
at the end of the day
it changes my hardened face
for just one beautiful moment

*

I carry you
I carry myself
I've always been good at carrying

WATERLILY GARDEN

He dreamt
of a waterlily garden
When he woke
I saw golden fish
still swimming
in the ponds of his eyes

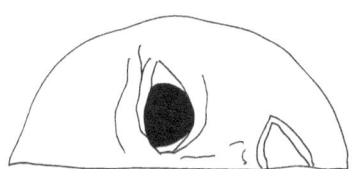

FROM THE LIGHT OF MY HEART

From the light of my heart
I cast a shadow
In that darkness
I find you
V i s h n u

MY WOMB IS EGYPT

A might in my body
Is pushing you out

Suddenly, I understand
That the only way you can grow
Is by leaving me

I ache like the wilderness
My womb is Egypt

THIS IS CALLED DESIRE

From one day to the next
You want things
This is called desire
But do not be afraid my baby
Like I have been
Instead, soothe yourself
With a creator's delight
Desire is a bonfire
Of paradisical light

TO BE BORN YOU HAVE TO TRUDGE THROUGH FILTH

To be born, you have to trudge through filth
You have to purify somebody
Take them in your arms
Pretend to be their child
Love them
You have to look on what is clean and spit on it
You have to find solitude in her body
Wonder at the world like a fool
Seek the light like a prisoner
Separate yourself from God
Find a way
To make him whole again

I LOVE HIM IN A GARDEN

I love him in a garden
With his shining black eyes
His stained, runaway fingers
Working hard in the gold, damp light
He toils for his deepest nature
Profoundly hidden from his sight
His hands feel like burning ice
When they dig out my pounding heart

THE FEELING OF HIS SHINING

My heart blazes
like a candle
the whole night through
I dream without sleep
The feeling of his shining
keeps me awake

PARADISE IS AT THE FEET OF MOTHER

I returned to the earth
The insides of my body
I licked my blood, like rain
I dug into the soul of the soil
Where we arrive into her arms

Paradise is at the feet of Mother

IT'S RIGHT TO BE ALONE

Now and then
It's right to be alone
It strips away the mother
Lets Sinai happen
Again and again
Makes way
For an effortless woman
To emerge from the waste
And calm God down
In all his masculine rage

LITTLE BIRD

Little bird
Feeding from my marble hand
I am a graven image
Witnessing your perfect plan
Humbled by
Your helpless sparrow mouth
My fingers
Have never felt so holy

HIGHER MOTHER

Every night
Reluctant and relieved
I hand you over
Into the arms
Of a higher Mother
You wave
Floating into the far away
Until you are a grain of sand
Barely visible on her naked breast

FAILURE, YOU MAKE ME PROUD

Even though I feel revealed
I know my beauty
is completely unseen now

*

In my stupor
I can still feel
his simple power
on my fingertips
from our last caress

*

Failure,
you make me proud
of everything I never was
and everything I'll never be

*

It's hard to believe
he won't remember any of this
but I won't forget

THE SNAKE MADE US EAT

The snake made us eat
From the tree of waking up
But you are just a baby
To drink from that cup

Keep sleeping my baby
There is much time to waste
Let the serpent take rest
'til it begs for your taste

YOU'VE MADE ME FORGET MY OWN BEAUTY

You've made me forget my own beauty
What a relief
To flop and fade
And fall away
In the sheer ecstasy
Of becoming
No one

YOU ARE STILL FRAGRANT

You are still fragrant
Of the garden
Whence you came:
Sour apples
And holy petals
That still ache
For the touch of your skin

IF YOU HEAR A BIRD

I want to touch
everything he has touched
his caresses
have made my life holy

Look how we are rewarded
for pleasure
yet we continue
to believe otherwise

If you hear a bird
love just happened
if you write a song
longing is everything

MANY THINGS MUST DIE

Many things must die
So one thing can live
Life is very simple now
I can only sit here and let this happen

When I kiss him, even my lips ache
I am torn and beaten to a delightful pulp

My blood has changed
I no longer feel the cold
I am always warm in his ravenous light

I am learning how to breathe
How to walk, how to speak
We are being born at exactly the same time

YOU HAVE MANY SECRET NAMES

You were born
From all the parts of my body

You have faith in us
Not the other way around

Human is only one of your names
You have many secret names

IMPRINT OF YOU

An astonishing void
Is within me
But this womb
Can never be empty
From the imprint of you

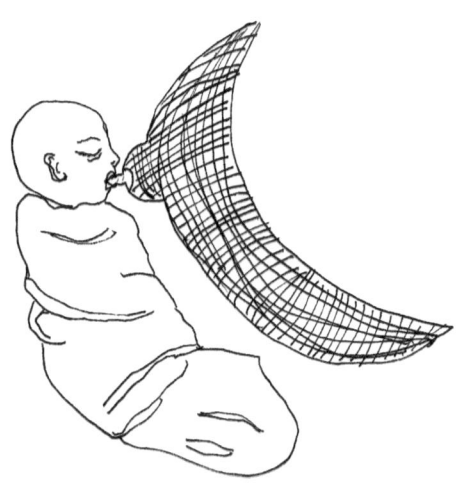

ALL MY WRONG BECOMES A FLOWER

All my wrong becomes a flower
Growing in your wild
Let me live around your neck
Like a garland for the gods

MILK IS MORE REAL THAN RAIN

The bitter herbs of my heart
Become honey in his mouth
His innocence swallows my mistakes
Turns them into grace

He takes me in his arms
Sees me as I am
I do not know my own secrets
Milk is more real than rain

IN THE WORLD YET TO COME

When you were born
My tongue was tied
With trembling and joy
How do I live now that I can speak?

*

You wake us at dawn
To pray with the rising sun
This will birth the messiah
Living in our hearts

*

There is a new rage within me
It catches me by surprise
I rest assured
God makes everything beautiful in its time

*

I like knowing words are waiting for me
At the end of the day
When I touch emptiness
I appear to be a person with strength

*

In the world yet to come
There is rest for us all
In that palace
We realise that we are all mothers

*

It is a great relief
That I matter so little now
I am scraps on your bedroom floor
I am a saved man

THE LORD ALWAYS HEARS
A CRY IN THE NIGHT

The night you were born
In the black of the light
I became a man
Licking the earth with delight

And in that darkness
Two snakes began a fight
They bit my womb once
They bit my womb twice

And in that blood
And in that rite
Came sound after sound
And cry after cry

All distress turns to strength
In the black of the light
The Lord always hears
A cry in the night

I FEEL HER MAGNET

Standing by her shore
Mother and child
We feel her magnet

See how pure our faces look
When she sweeps away our dreams
And we are left with nothing

YOU MUST NOT KNOW YOURSELF

You must be concealed to be revealed
You must not know yourself
To find a perfect moment

*

There is no God
Until God becomes Mother
Until then, nothing can be born

*

Everything comes out of barrenness
The desert is full of flowers
Yet we don't even notice

*

We are born humble as the trees
But don't you want to find out
What is underneath your humility?

LIONHEART

I didn't know
that the letting go
would need to happen
so immediately
I thought
we had years

Suddenly
from birth
I must
give you wings

You are just
a tiny spark
I will need
a Lionheart
for this

I WISH YOU THOUGHT I WAS BEAUTIFUL

This is my body
This is my blood
Which I have given up
For him

Take and eat
Of this heavy, limp thing
I wish you thought I was beautiful

THIS IS WHERE WE MEET
*(where I fall at the feet of Mother and weep
bitterly for all the lost things)*

I said
Mother, how do I find you
Now that I am always with him?

She said
Every time you pick him up
And bend your body to him
This is your new worship
This is where we meet

But I said
Mother, what about my own needs
Now that I am only with him?

And she said
Surrender your preferences
These are your new prayers
This is where we meet

And I said
Mother, I have no time for you
Now that I am only with him?

And she said
Sacrifice your thoughts into his fire
Time is eternal there
This is where we meet

HIS RIVER IS NOT FILLED WITH WATER

He names every bird in the garden
His words come from a secret in his heart
So that every name sounds like a song to the gods

This is how he creates the world
With names
Until then, nothing exists

His river is not filled with water
It is full of the sweet wine of compassion

I AM A VINE

I am a vine
And he is my branches
Apart from me
He can do nothing
    *

Union is the most natural thing of all
We had to learn
How to become two
    *

Watching him from a distance
In the arms of other people
I recover something that is gone
Or coming
Or never coming back
    *

There is only one moment that is mine
When I sit here with you
And hold my feelings to the light

I FOUND HIM IN A BASKET

I found him in a basket
In the milk of a flowing river
He took me to the mountain
Where the rocks cry out and quiver
We were shown the face of Mother
The giver of eternal life
She unveiled her flickering love
In the blade of a rusty knife
I wept in her jagged arms
I hid in her perfumed leaves
As she sang me the song of mothers
'By giving, she receives'
And she sang me the song of all mothers
'By giving, she receives'

A MYSTERY I CAN'T REMEMBER NOW

The ocean is loud, but it fills my heart with
a strange silence.

When he drank rain in the garden, I suddenly
understood a mystery that I can't remember now.

Even though his eyes are as dark as midnight,
he sees through everything, everyone.

Slowly, I die but no one seems to notice.

I WILL NEVER PRAY WITH MY EYES CLOSED AGAIN

I will never pray
With my eyes closed again
Blessed be my eyes
Born to behold
This unbridled beauty

YOU BELONG TO THE FEMININE

You belong to the feminine
Because seeds belong to woman
Whoever you are
I know you
You reveal me
You always will

Photograph by Romina Mandrini

JESSICA CHAPNIK KAHN is an Argentinian Australian singer-songwriter, author and actor who has worked in theatre, tv and film. As a musician she has released two solo albums under the moniker Appleonia and worked with some of Australia's finest artists. As a writer she has published the children's book *Lenny and the Ants* and co-authored the biography *A Repurposed Life*, which was nominated for an ABIA award for Biography Book of the Year. *MADRE* is her first collection of poetry.

www.ingramcontent.com/pod-product-compliance
Lightning Source LLC
Chambersburg PA
CBHW030040100526
44590CB00011B/275